CREATE IN ME
A PURE HEART

ANSWERS FOR STRUGGLING WOMEN

2008 December

www.purelifeministries.org

888.PURELIFE

ALSO AVAILABLE BY STEVE GALLAGHER:

At the Altar of Sexual Idolatry
At the Altar of Sexual Idolatry Workbook
A Biblical Guide to Counseling the Sexual Addict
Create in Me a Pure Heart
How America Lost Her Innocence
Intoxicated with Babylon
Irresistible to God
A Lamp Unto My Feet
Living in Victory
Out of the Depths of Sexual Sin
Press ~~Toward~~ Heavenly Calling
The Walk of Repentance

For these books and other teaching materials please contact:

PURE LIFE MINISTRIES
14 School Street
Dry Ridge, KY 41035
(888) PURELIFE - to order
(859) 824-4444
(859) 813-0005 FAX
www.purelifeministries.org

CREATE IN ME A PURE HEART WORKBOOK
Copyright © 2007 by Steve and Kathy Gallagher.
All rights reserved. No part of this book may be reproduced
in any form except for brief quotations, without
written permission from the author.

ISBN 0-9758832-8-3
EAN 978-0-9758832-8-0

CREATE IN ME A PURE HEART

ANSWERS FOR STRUGGLING WOMEN

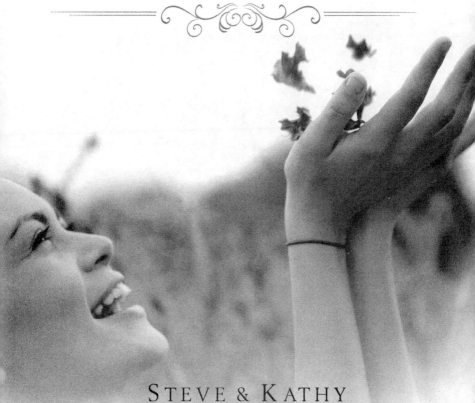

STEVE & KATHY
GALLAGHER

CONTENTS

VISIT THE CREATE IN ME A PURE HEART BLOG

and Journal Your Thoughts as You Read

We have created a special blog for this book. Its purpose is to be a place for you to share what the Lord is doing in your life as you read. Each chapter will have posts by Kathy Gallagher, as well as links to free resources that will further minister to you. Stop by to post your own thoughts or to just read what others are saying for your own encouragement. Either way, it's there for you at:

www.purelifeministries.org/pureheartblog

INTRODUCTION

The purpose of this workbook is to help the reader of *Create in Me a Pure Heart* to focus on the major themes presented in each chapter. In doing so, the reader can expect to gain a better understanding of the issues and truths discussed throughout the book. While reading alone is helpful, having to search for the answers to questions and then write them down will enhance one's retention of the important steps provided for overcoming sexual sin.

With that in mind, several questions have been generated from each of the seventeen chapters. You will find that we often quoted sentences which contain the answer to a particular question. The questions are also arranged in accordance with the order in which the chapters were written. For instance, the answer to question number 7 will always be located in the chapter somewhere between the answers to questions 6 and 8.

Finding the answers will not always be easy. You may have to go back and forth over portions of the text. That's the way it is supposed to be! The more you have to search for answers, the more likely the material of the book is going to "get into you." If you should come across a question that you just cannot find the answer to, skip it until you have completed the entire workbook. Then, *only as a last resort*, you can look up the answer in the back of the book. If you look it up while you are still in the chapter, you will not be able to find that answer without seeing the other answers for that chapter. This would only serve to defeat the whole purpose of this exercise.

The answers to the scriptural questions are not provided. There are two reasons for this. First, people use different translations of the Bible, which will affect the way the answer reads. Secondly, most of the answers will be based upon the reader's own perspective. Please keep in mind that we use the New American Standard version of the Bible and some of the questions reflect the wording of that translation.

You will experience a wide range of feelings as you read *Create in Me a Pure Heart*. Sometimes it will be painful, while other times will be filled with hope as you sense God's loving presence there to help you. Make notes as you go through this. One day it will be a real blessing to look back at the different spiritual and emotional experiences you have during this special time in your life.

I hope this workbook is a blessing to you as you seek the biblical answers for your needs.

STEVE AND KATHY GALLAGHER

CHAPTER ONE:
WOMEN AND SEXUAL SIN

Study Questions

1. What two things did "all these women" share in common?

   a.

   b.

2. Complete the sentence which begins, "While there are those women who are simply addicted to some type of sexual activity…"

3. In this chapter, we listed three questions that were posed in a survey we conducted on the Pure Life Ministries website. Circle the answers that apply to you.

   1. Which of the following types of behavior regarding romance, past or present, have you been involved in?
      a. Entertaining romantic fantasies
      b. Reading romance novels
      c. Watching soap operas
      d. Establishing romantic relationships on the Internet
      e. Flirting with guys
      f. Frequent casual dating
      g. Watching romantic movies

   2. Which of the following types of behavior regarding pornography, past or present, have you been involved in?
      a. Viewing adult movies with another person
      b. Viewing adult movies alone
      c. Occasionally viewing magazines/Internet pornography
      d. Regularly viewing magazines/Internet pornography
      e. Reading pornographic stories

   3. Which of the following types of behavior regarding sexual sin, past or present, have you been involved in?
      a. Masturbation
      b. Online sexual conversations
      c. Promiscuity/fornication with other singles
      d. Affair(s)
      e. Straight but having bisexual experiences
      f. Homosexual lifestyle
      g. Involved in the adult entertainment industry

4. Describe in your own words the change that came over Susan's perspectives about pornography. What was her initial attitude toward it, and how did this attitude change with repeated exposure to it?

5. What did Jill deceive herself about?

6. The U.S. Centers for Disease Control and Prevention prepared reports about homosexual activity among women in 1992 and 2005. What percentage of women in all age groups had had sexual encounters with other women?

   a. 1992:

   b. 2005:

What the Scriptures Say

1. Read the following verses and write down what you learn about sin:

Proverbs 5:22

Proverbs 7:22-23

Proverbs 26:11

2. Read II Peter 2:9-22 and answer the following questions.

   In verse 9, Peter describes the "godly" and the "unrighteous." In the rest of the chapter, he lists a number of characteristics of the unrighteous. Write down ten of these characteristics.

   a.   b.

c.   d.

e.   f.

g.   h.

i.   j.

Write out verses 18 and 19.

Explain what you think Peter is saying in verse 21.

Personal Examination

1. What did you learn about women in sexual sin from this chapter?

2. What did you learn about yourself from this chapter?

Group Discussion Questions

1. Could you relate to the desperation of the woman who wrote the email? If so, how?
2. Were you surprised at the types of sexual sin Christian women are involved in?
3. Did you ever feel as though you were the only one with your problem? Has that changed?
4. Which woman mentioned in this chapter could you most relate to? Why?
5. Without being too specific, how did your problems with sexual sin begin?

CHAPTER TWO:
ROMANCE AND THE EMOTIONAL CONNECTION

Study Questions

1. What was Tiffany's initial fantasy and where did it come from?

2. How did that fantasy set her up for the online activities she eventually became involved in?

3. Complete the sentence which begins, "Certainly it is common and natural…"

4. What did Kay Arthur become in her search for love?

5. What was Gloria "needy for" and how did it affect her if she didn't receive it?

6. Complete the sentence which begins, "Instead of entering marriage…"

7. How did Vicky's unreal expectations of marriage set her up for her own failures?

8. Write out the two lies we quoted from Nancy DeMoss's book:

Lie # 32:

Lie # 33:

What the Scriptures Say

1. Read Galatians 5:16-25 and answer the following questions.

According to Galatians 5:16, what would you say is the answer to overcoming the temptation to sin?

List three things you can do to help you to "walk in the Spirit."

a.

b.

c.

Ponder the list provided in Galatians 5:19-21. Examine your heart and the actions of your life. Write down any of these "deeds of the flesh" which are at work in your life.

Write out Galatians 5:24.

Personal Examination

1. What did you learn about romantic fantasies in this chapter?

2. What did you learn about yourself in this chapter?

Group Discussion Questions

1. What is the danger of entertaining romantic fantasies?
2. Have you had an inappropriate desire to be connected emotionally with another person?
3. Compare the stories of Tiffany and Robin. How did their romantic fantasies affect them similarly?
4. Did Kay Arthur's confession surprise you? What does her story tell you about the power of repentance?
5. How do men and women tend to differ in their emotional and sexual lives?

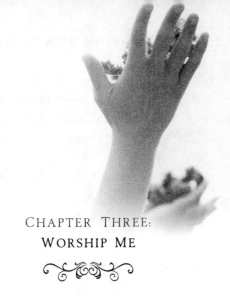

CHAPTER THREE:
WORSHIP ME

Study Questions

1. Complete the sentence which begins, "The truth is that prosperity…"

2. What are "trendy shows such as *Friends, The OC, One Tree Hill,*" teaching girls?

3. According to one study, how many cases of "sexually transmitted diseases among teens" are there annually?

4. What are "defense mechanisms?"

5. What did Latisha love?

6. What was Lisa "oblivious" to?

7. What did Lisa want?

8. According to Bob Harrington, what do strippers on Bourbon Street " soon fall prey to?"

What the Scriptures Say

1. Read I Timothy 2:9-10 and I Peter 3:3-5. In your own words, combine and rewrite these passages into one comprehensive statement.

2. According to I Timothy 2:9-10, what did Paul want for
    Christian women?

3. In your own words, explain the eternal implications of
    Peter's statement in I Peter 3:3-5.

Personal Examination

1. What did you learn about women desiring male attention from this chapter?

2. What did you learn about yourself from this chapter?

Group Discussion Questions

1. What are your feelings about the growing cosmetic surgery trend among women?
2. Why do you feel this trend is gaining momentum in America?
3. What is at the root of the desire to be seen as beautiful?
4. What part does pride play in this desire?
5. Do you ever dress in a certain way to gain the attention of men?

CHAPTER FOUR:
LUST, FANTASY AND MASTURBATION

Study Questions

1. What similar problem did Carole, Stacey and Peggy face
   that contributed to them becoming involved in sexual sin?

2. Complete the sentence which begins, "The truth is that a
   woman…"

3. What will "the one who is looking for the path of least resistance in life" lack?

4. Complete the sentence which begins, "Just as the physical heart pumps life-giving blood..."

5. Write out the three definitions provided for the Greek word *epithumeo*.

    a.

    b.

    c.

6. Describe the "two primary categories" of lust.

    a.

    b.

7. What did Jesus face when He "began His ministry in Israel?"

8. Complete the sentence which begins, "He said exactly what He meant…"

9. Complete the sentence which begins, "For instance, if we are talking about…"

10. When would the word stumble not be "the appropriate term to use?"

11. Complete the sentence which begins, "While occasions do exist wherein believers remain needlessly old-fashioned regarding particular issues…"

12. Who views "sex as simply one room in the vast pleasure palace of life?"

What The Scriptures Say

1. Write out five of the verses about the human heart listed on page 65.

   a.

   b.

   c.

   d.

   e.

2. Read the following verses and explain in your own words what you learn about lust.

   Proverbs 6:25

Job 31:1

Matthew 5:27-28

II Peter 2:14a

3. Proverbs 7 describes how a harlot seduces a young man
    walking down the street. Rewrite a condensed version
    of this chapter in your own words substituting Internet
    pornography for the harlot. How would it approach
    you? How would it seduce you? What could the
    consequences be?

Personal Examination

1. What did you learn about lust from this chapter?

2. What did you learn about masturbation from this chapter?

3. Do you feel more convicted about the wrongness of lust and masturbation than you did before reading this chapter?

Group Discussion Questions

1. Has this chapter altered your perspectives on the sinfulness of lust? If so, how?
2. Has this chapter altered your perspectives on the sinfulness of masturbation? If so, how?
3. What insights have you gained on the make-up of the human heart?
4. How do you feel the world's attitudes regarding sexuality have influenced the Church's overall mindset regarding this subject?
5. Discuss how the average believer today would differ in his viewpoints about pornography and sexual sin from the typical Christian of a century ago.

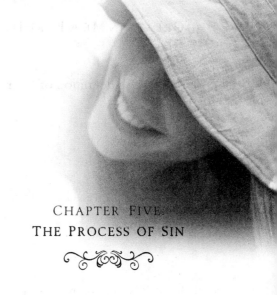

CHAPTER FIVE:
THE PROCESS OF SIN

Study Questions

1. Describe the "complex chain of actions" which those who are bound up in habitual sexual sin are actually addicted to.

2. What does "honey" represent?

3. What does "smooth oil" represent?

CREATE IN ME A PURE HEART WORKBOOK

4. Give Jenson's definition of "a trigger."

5. What are the "three circumstances that usually" prove disastrous?

   a.

   b.

   c.

6. Can you see how these three circumstances have affected your ability to withstand temptation? Explain your answer.

7. Why are "these thoughts...difficult to control?"

8. According to Dietrich Bonhoeffer, what does Satan fill us with?

9. In your own words describe how people fool themselves when "moving toward sin."

10. What takes over "once the body is in motion?"

11. From your own experience, why is the actual act of sin so often a disappointment?

12. Write out three resolutions that you have made in the past.

   a.

   b.

   c.

13. How can you prepare now to face future temptations in your specific area of struggle?

What the Scriptures Say

1. Read James 1:13-16 and answer the following questions.

   Why do you think some people might say, "I am being tempted by God?"

   In light of your own experience, what do you think that James meant when he said that a person who is tempted "is carried away and enticed by his [or her] own lust?"

2. Read Proverbs 5:3-13 and answer the following questions.

   What is Solomon's main piece of advice in this section of scripture?

What are the five things that will happen if you do not heed this advice?

a.

b.

c.

d.

e.

Personal Examination

1. What did you learn about the process of sin from this chapter?

2. What did you learn about your own sin from this chapter?

Group Discussion Questions

1. How have you responded to temptation in the past?
2. How have "the three circumstances" affected your ability to withstand temptation? (see p. 77-78)
3. Have you ever insisted on keeping a job which "made provision for the flesh?"
4. What is the difference between a resolution and repentance?
5. Discuss the truth of I Corinthians 10:13.

CHAPTER SIX:
THE ROOT ISSUES

Study Questions

1. Explain in your own words how humanistic mercy and God's mercy would differ in their approaches to Pam's problems with sexual sin.

2. What does the Bible teach "the struggling woman to deal with?"

3. Complete the sentence which begins, "The truth is, before…"

4. What is "the first step toward victory?"

5. What is "one of the justifications we have heard over the years?"

6. Complete the sentence which begins, "Since the roots of the person's…"

7. According to many psychologists, what lies "behind every human dilemma?"

8. What does "habitual sexual sin" stem from?

9. According to Romans 8:29, what is God's great purpose in the life of a believer?

10. What "way of life" must the sexual addict embrace to find victory over sin?

11. According to the authors, what is pride?

12. List the eight different variations of pride.

    a.

    b.

    c.

    d.

    e.

    f.

    g.

    h.

What the Scriptures Say

1. Read the following verses and write down what you learn about pride and humility.

    Psalm 101:5

Psalm 138:6

James 4:10

Romans 12:3

Romans 12:16

Luke 22:26

2. Consider what you have learned about the different kinds of pride and what you have learned in the Bible about the importance of humility. Pick out three types of pride that you struggle with and describe how they affect those around you and why you feel it is important to allow God to work them out of your life.

3. Read Luke 9:22-25 and answer the following questions.

   According to verse 22, what did the King of kings have to look forward to?

   According to verse 23, what are the three things His followers should do?

According to verses 24 and 25, what will happen to the man who attempts to "save his life?"

Personal Examination

1. What did you learn about the roots of sexual addiction from this chapter?

2. What did you learn about yourself from this chapter?

Group Discussion Questions

1. Have you ever had the attitude that you have your problems because of what someone else did or did not do to you?
2. Discuss why it is so important to understand and embrace God's perspective of mercy rather than man's.
3. Read and discuss Luke 9:22-25.
4. Can you relate to any of the different types of pride?
5. Why is it important for God to humble us?

CHAPTER SEVEN

THE NEED TO LIVE IN THE LIGHT

Study Questions

1. What are the three reasons given which help to motivate women to "maintain secrecy about their sin?"

   a.

   b.

   c.

2. In your own words, describe the term "inside world."

3. What is said about "the deepest part of our inner man?"

4. In what ways have you been "outward" around other Christians?

5. Complete the three following statements or phrases about the progression of fear.

    a. Presumably it begins…

    b. The fear is deepened…

    c. and becomes embedded…

6. Complete the sentence which begins, "In essence, they ignore…"

7. What is a person saying, in essence, when she "blameshifts, minimizes or conceals her sin?"

8. What will the woman eventually discover "who thinks she can continue hiding her sin?"

9. In your own words, explain the "correlation between a person's involvement with sin and her awareness of it."

10. Complete the sentence which begins, "Keeping herself hyped…"

11. How would you respond to people who say they "could not bear to hurt" their spouses who are unaware of their sexual sin?

12. Read the final section of this chapter and describe in your own words the difference between accountability and discipleship.

What the Scriptures Say

1. Read Luke 12:1-5 and answer the following questions.

   What are the three things which Jesus commands us to do in this passage of Scripture?

   a.

   b.

   c.

   Describe what hypocrisy has to do with things which are "covered up" and "hidden," and words spoken "in the dark" and "whispered in the inner rooms."

   Read this passage of Scripture over again carefully. In your own words, what would you say that Jesus is saying to the reader?

Personal Examination

1. What did you learn about living in the light from this chapter?

2. What did you learn about yourself from this chapter?

Group Discussion Questions

1. Have you ever kept sin hidden? Why?
2. Have you ever experienced God lovingly exposing your secret sin?
3. Have you attempted to make yourself look as though you were doing better than you really were spiritually?
4. Can you see how sin deceives the heart?
5. Have you humbled yourself to be discipled by someone more mature than you are?

CHAPTER EIGHT:
FREEDOM COMES SLOWLY
FOR A REASON

Study Questions

1. In what two ways does God transform a woman?

    a.

    b.

2. How does the Lord usually deal "with those in sexual sin?"

3. Complete the sentence which begins, "One of the things…"

4. In your own words, how would you say that God uses a woman's sin to "eventually draw her closer to Himself?"

5. Complete the sentence which begins, "God is often more…"

6. In the section called "God's Timing," the woman who has been "set free from her sin" is asked three questions. Write out these questions, but instead of writing the word "her," personalize each question. We will give the first one as an example.

    a. Will my selfishness simply be transferred to spending money?

    b.

    c.

7. What life "is not spared the experience of pain?"

8. Give the five "synonyms for the word conquer."

    a.   b.

    c.   d.

    e.

9. In Old Testament times, the Lord required the Israelites to war against the idolatrous nations around them. Explain in your own words why the Lord would want you to learn to battle against your own flesh.

10. Write out (and answer for yourself) the four questions regarding "how long it will take" to receive victory over sin.

    a.

    b.

c.

d.

11. Does habitual sin seem like a mountain for you to overcome? Do you see how using the biblical steps outlined in this book could help you conquer that mountain? Write out a statement of determination, that with God's help, you will overcome.

What the Scriptures Say

1. Read II Corinthians 4:16-18 and answer the following questions.

The Apostle Paul suffered greatly during his years of ministry. Considering these verses, why do you think he had so much joy in life?

What would you say is the importance of your inner man "being renewed day by day?"

Considering verse 18, what was Paul fixing his attention on?

Write out Colossians 3:1-2

Personal Examination

1. What did you learn about why it takes time to come into freedom?

2. What did you learn about what you can expect for yourself after reading this chapter?

Group Discussion Questions

1. Spend your time discussing the reasons why freedom comes slowly:
   a. If we were freed instantly, we might not appreciate our freedom.
   b. The process teaches us to rely upon God.
   c. God is very concerned that we mature as Christians also during this period of restoration.
   d. God wants us to learn to battle the desires of the flesh.

CHAPTER NINE:
HOW MUCH DO YOU CARE?

Study Questions

1. Explain what advantage there is to seeing the life of someone who has overcome habitual sin.

2. Complete the sentence which begins, "You may have blamed…"

3. How would you relate the boxer illustration to your need to change?

4. In your own words, explain the "If-Then Principle."

5. What "was established by God as the means to receiving His help?"

6. How would you compare your situation to the history of "the nation of Israel?"

7. Who is "the center of the Christian faith?"

8. What is our faith "inextricably tied to?"

9. What is "one of the terrible and frightening aspects of sin?"

10. Take a few minutes to write out your own "believing prayer."

What the Scriptures Say

1. I (Steve) once did a Bible study that greatly affected my life. The conviction had been growing within me that "our faith is inextricably tied to who He is." Everything in our lives hinges on our trust in God. With this in mind, look up the following verses and, just to get a fuller picture of this, replace the word faith with the phrase, "the knowledge of the good and merciful character of God." I'll do the first one as an example.

Matthew 6:30

> "But if God so arrays the grass of the field, which is alive today and tomorrow is thrown into the furnace, will He not much more do so for you, O men of little *knowledge of the good and merciful character of God?*"

Habakkuk 2:4

Matthew 9:22

Romans 10:17

II Corinthians 5:7

I Timothy 6:10

James 1:3

James 1:6

I Peter 1:7

I John 5:4

Personal Examination

1. What did you learn about having a sincere desire for victory from this chapter?

2. What did you learn about your own level of determination from this chapter?

Group Discussion Questions

1. Read and discuss Luke 11:5-8 in light of desiring victory over sin.
2. Read and discuss Luke 18:1-7 in light of desiring victory over sin.
3. Do you ever struggle with wanting to overcome badly enough to do what it takes to get that victory?
4. Discuss faith in the context of one's intimate, personal relationship with God.
5. How does your trust in Him affect your cry for help?

CHAPTER TEN:
THE SINFUL FLESH

Study Questions

1. What are "the three forces which work tirelessly to compel us toward sin?"

   a.   b.   c.

2. What is it that "God wants?"

3. Complete the sentence which begins, "An alcoholic could go..."

4. What are the three things the flesh (or physical nature) "is only interested in?"

     a.   b.

     c.

5. What is "every human being" born with?

6. What words are used by the Bible to describe the inner man?

7. How does "the wide variety of outside stimuli" enter a person's mind?

8. Complete the sentence which begins, "Just as the flesh grows…"

9. Practice is an important element in the process of changing our habits. Complete the following three sentences:

a. "If we practice (or sow) ungodliness..."

b. "By the same token, if we practice godliness..."

c. "Feelings always..."

10. What is "the primary enemy we will face?"

What the Scriptures Say

1. Read the sixth chapter of Romans and answer the following questions.

   In verse 7 Paul says: "for he who has died is freed from sin." There are two perspectives on this. Some think that it means that a believer can no longer be bound by sin. He simply must accept this "truth" by faith and the sin will go away. We agree with others that what Paul is saying is that the believer has been freed from the *legal authority* sin once had over him. He "has been bought with a price..." He is now a child of God and sin can have no dominion over him that he does not allow it to have. Whereas, before he came to the Lord he was completely subject to sin, now the power of God is available to him to free him from habitual sin. Carefully examine Romans chapters six, seven and eight. Do you see anything in these chapters which expresses the idea that a person becomes freed from sin by "believing" he is free?

What are the commands given in 6:12-13?

2. Read Romans 8:5-8 and describe in your own words what Paul is teaching.

3. In I Corinthians 2:16 Paul makes the statement, "But we have the mind of Christ." Again, these same teachers say that the Apostle was making a blanket statement of fact and the mind of Christ will be ours as we "accept it by faith." We propose another perspective: Believers have *access* to the mind of Christ and can enter into His thinking, perspectives and compassion as they mature in the faith. Read the following verses and write down a

simple "yes" or "no" to whether or not you believe the
Corinthians had the mind of Christ.

I Corinthians 1:11-12

I Corinthians 3:1-4

Paul had the mind of Christ because he lived an extremely
consecrated life. People can claim to have the mind of
Christ, but the reality of it is proven through their love,
humility, and godliness; not through presumptuous
assertions.

4. Read Hebrews 11:6. Would you say that faith has more to
    do with a personal, daily trust in God or in the acceptance
    of doctrinal beliefs expressed by men?

5. There are over 1,000 commands given to the believer in
    the New Testament. Would you say that God is looking
    for us to live godly, consecrated lives?

Personal Examination

1. What did you learn about the importance of overcoming the desires of the flesh from this chapter?

2. What did you learn about your own nature from this chapter?

Group Discussion Questions

1. Read and discuss the struggles Paul expressed in Romans 7:15-25.
2. Can you relate to these battles within?
3. Discuss how habits play such a prominent part in our daily lives.
4. How could one establish new habits?

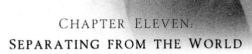

CHAPTER ELEVEN:
SEPARATING FROM THE WORLD

Study Questions

1. Complete the sentence which begins, "With such overwhelming…"

2. Write out the statement of Lester Sumrall.

3. What has "God called us to" do?

4. What does Dr. Jenson say to Christians who claim that television "does not affect" them?

5. Answer the following rhetorical questions asked in the book:

   "How does the pleasure-is-everything mindset propagated by television affect a Christian woman's need for inner sobriety?"

   "What is the cumulative effect of seeing sexual innuendos night after night on TV?"

"How is she affected when she accumulates countless hours watching situation comedies that mock everything which is decent?"

6. According to Don Wildmon, what is "the greatest educator we have?"

7. What image does Peter's exhortation to "be sober and vigilant" create in one's mind?

8. Complete the two following statements:

"Rather than aggressively tearing down the strongholds of the enemy and waging war for the souls of our loved ones..."

"Instead of affecting the world around us for the cause of Christ..."

What the Scriptures Say

1. Read Matthew 7:13. Would you say that those who are subjecting themselves to the spirit of this world are on the narrow path or the broad way?

2. Read II Corinthians 6:14-7:1 and answer the following questions.

    In verse 14, Paul uses three descriptive terms describing the relationship we should not have with unbelievers. In the NASB, they are "bound," "partnership," and "fellowship." What are they in your translation (if it is different)?

    What does God command of His people in verse 17?

    What three things does He promise in verses 17 and 18 to those who will do this?

    a.

    b.

    c.

Write out II Corinthians 7:1.

3. Read Romans 12:1-2 and answer the following questions.

What does Paul command us to do in the first verse?

In verse 2 he commands us not to "be conformed to this world." List three ways you feel that you are still conformed to this world.

a.

b.

c.

Personal Examination

1. What did you learn about separating from the world from this chapter?

2. What did you learn about your own love for this world from this chapter?

Group Discussion Questions

1. What are some ways the spirit of this world can affect your life?
2. Read and discuss II Corinthians 6:14-7:1 and its ramifications for today's Christian.
3. Discuss Wildmon's allegation that television is basically defaming Christians. (see p. 164-165)
4. How do you feel the Internet has affected the level of your consecration to God?
5. How do you feel the world's values about life differ from those expressed in Scripture?

CHAPTER TWELVE:
BATTLES IN THE SPIRITUAL REALM

Study Questions

1. In your own words describe the teachings about spiritual warfare which are at the two "opposite end[s] of the spectrum."

    a.

    b.

2. Complete the following sentences or phrases:

    "To the one who struggles with depression…"

    "For those who battle a hot temper…"

"for an exaggerated sex drive..."

3. Give a brief explanation of the spiritual law in Galatians 6:7-8.

4. Give a brief explanation of the spiritual law in
    Matthew 23:12.

5. What is "the primary point of" John's statement?

6. According to Dr. Unger, what happens when a believer
    yields to "pressure, suggestion, and temptation?"

7. Would you say that the enemy or demons can attack believers in whatever way and to whatever degree they wish? Explain your answer.

8. Describe in your own words how a stronghold is created within a person.

9. Who is it who has a "vague concept" of victory?

10. Explain in your own words "the place of refuge for the believer."

What the Scriptures Say

1. Read Ephesians 6:10-18 and answer the following questions.

    According to verse 10, where does our strength come from?

    According to verse 11, why should we "put on the full armor of God?"

    What are the four enemies listed in verse 12?

    a.

    b.

    c.

    d.

    In verses 14-17 there are six articles of armor with corresponding spiritual disciplines aligned with each. List each spiritual discipline and describe in your own words how you feel that it would help you to "stand firm against the schemes of the devil."

a.

b.

c.

d.

e.

f.

2. Read John 14:30 and explain in your own words why this is or is not true of you.

Personal Examination

1. What did you learn about spiritual warfare from this chapter?

2. What did you learn about your own struggles with the enemy from this chapter?

Group Discussion Questions

1. Can you think of any temptation to fall into sin you have encountered in the past which you are fairly certain the enemy arranged?
2. Read II Corinthians 10:3-6 and discuss the implications of these verses.
3. Read the illustration about Joseph (using Job's story) and discuss what conversations might have occurred between the devil and God about you. (see p. 179)
4. Have different women read the following verses: II Corinthians 2:11; 11:3; 11:14-15; I Peter 5:8. Discuss what you learn about the enemy from these verses.

CHAPTER THIRTEEN:
THE PLACE OF BROKENNESS
AND REPENTANCE

Study Questions

1. What is "the answer for the woman struggling with sexual sin?"

2. How does this change come about?

3. What must take place "in order for God to get a woman to the place where she is able to forsake the idols of her life?"

4. Regarding the human will, what "is sheer nonsense?"

5. Complete the sentence which begins, "*Spiritual repentance is…*"

6. Explain in your own words the difference between Zacchaeus and the man who agreed to follow Jesus but first wanted to say good-bye to those at home.

7. What is it that "repentance describes?"

8. In your own words, describe what part being "poor in spirit" plays in the process of the repentance of sin.

9. In your own words, describe what part "mourning" plays in the process of the repentance of sin.

10. In your own words, describe what part "meekness" plays in the process of the repentance of sin.

What the Scriptures Say

1. Read the following verses and write down what you learn about God's will:

Matthew 7:21

Matthew 12:50

Matthew 26:42

John 7:17

Ephesians 6:6

I Thessalonians 4:3-5

Personal Examination

1. What did you learn about repentance from this chapter?

2. What did you learn about your own will from this chapter?

Group Discussion Questions

1. Have different woman read a beautitude and discuss its
    place in the process of repentance:

    vs. 3   Blessed are the poor in spirit, for theirs is the
            kingdom of heaven.

    vs. 4   Blessed are those who mourn, for they shall
            be comforted.

    vs. 5   Blessed are the gentle, for they shall inherit the earth.

    vs. 6   Blessed are those who hunger and thirst for
            righteousness, for they shall be satisfied.

    vs. 7   Blessed are the merciful, for they shall receive mercy.

    vs. 8   Blessed are the pure in heart, for they shall see God.

    vs. 9   Blessed are the peacemakers, for they shall be called
            sons of God.

CHAPTER FOURTEEN:
DISCIPLINED FOR HOLINESS

Study Questions

1. What does the Bible use "the term fool to describe?"

2. Read the letter to Lucy and explain in your own words how
    it is that someone can seem to be receiving the "blessings
    of God" and yet not even be saved.

3. Explain how the illustration about the man with the broken arm who would not go to the doctor relates to your own life (if it does).

4. What can one "readily distinguish" from "these passages?"

5. When Jesus rebuked Peter, what was "His only concern?"

6. Complete the sentence which begins, "Sometimes a sharp…"

7. If you were "to spend some time reading the epistles of
    First and Second Peter," what would you "read?"

8. What is "the problem with this sort of thinking?"

9. What "thinking is sheer fantasy?"

10. How does holiness come?

What the Scriptures Say

1. Write out in your own words what you learn about fools
    from the following verses:

    Proverbs 1:7

Proverbs 1:22

Proverbs 14:16

Proverbs 17:10

Proverbs 18:2

Proverbs 23:9

Ecclesiastes 7:4

2. Read Proverbs 5:7-13 and describe how this relates to your own life.

3. Read the following verses and explain in your own words
   what you learn about biblical discipline.

   Proverbs 12:1

   Proverbs 13:1

   Proverbs 13:18

   Proverbs 15:5

   Proverbs 15:31

   Proverbs 15:32

Personal Examination

1. What did you learn about God's process of discipline
   from this chapter?

2. What did you learn about your own reactions to His discipline from this chapter?

Group Discussion Questions

1. Discuss the "lifestyle of instant gratification, selfish indulgence, superficial relationships, and shallow commitments" we have been bombarded with and how it has encouraged sexual sin.
2. Can you see how the Lord was helping Peter through all the rebukes he received?
3. What do you suppose would have happened with Peter's life if he would have refused the correction God brought into his life?
4. Can you see how foolish it would be to go through life continually looking for a quick and painless solution to a problem that is rooted in one's character?

Study Questions

1. What must the woman do "if she wants to overcome habitual sin?"

2. Complete both halves of Paul's conditional promise.

    IF...

    THEN...

3. What would be the "modern day" term for *walk*?

4. "When Paul says to 'walk in the Spirit,' he is describing" what?

5. Read the section entitled, "The Daily Sustenance of Prayer" and, using the elements provided, write out a plan of action for establishing a prayer life.

What will be your "style" of prayer?

Where will you pray?

When will you pray?

How long will you pray each day?

How can you make worship a part of your prayer time?

6. Complete the sentence which begins, "One problem people in sexual sin…"

7. According to Dr. Jenson, what does it mean "to become 'transformed by the renewing of your mind?'"

8. What is it "we cannot emphasize enough?"

What the Scriptures Say

1. Read and pray over Galatians 5:19-21. Pick out three of these characteristics which apply to your life and describe your struggle with each.

    a.

    b.

    c.

2. Read James 1:21-25 and answer the following questions.

    What are the two things which you must put aside/lay apart/-get rid of before the word will be implanted?

    a.

    b.

    Write out verse 22.

What would you say it means to be a "doer of the word?"

According to verses 23 and 24, what happens to the person who "is a hearer of the word and not a doer?"

What does the person do who "shall be blessed in what he does?"

3. Read the following verses and tell in your own words what the word will do for the person who heeds it.

    Proverbs 2:10

    Proverbs 2:12

    Proverbs 6:23-24

    Proverbs 7:5

Personal Examination

1. What did you learn about walking in the Spirit from this chapter?

2. What did you learn about your own walk with God from this chapter?

Group Discussion Questions

1. What does it really mean to walk in the Spirit?
2. Read and discuss John 15:1-5.
3. What kind of problems do you have maintaining your devotional life?
4. How will a devotional life affect the person who struggles with habitual sin?
5. How will it help a struggling believer to really begin to live out the Word of God?

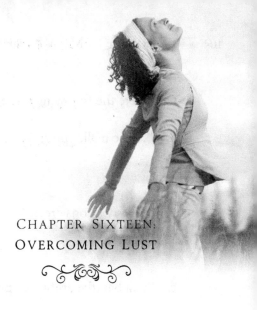

CHAPTER SIXTEEN:
OVERCOMING LUST

Study Questions

1. What must "the woman who is serious about walking in purity be willing" to do?"

2. What does "the spirit of this world" create?

3. Complete the sentence which begins, "In practical terms…"

4. Complete the following sentences:

   a. "…the mall…provokes…"

   b. "Beauty salons are…"

   c. "…a bar, the ambience puts her in a…"

5. What must the woman do "who is going to get the victory over lust?"

6. What is "hellish living?"

7. What is "one of the keys to bringing one's mind into subjection to the Spirit?"

8. What is "the feeling lodged within the grateful heart?"

9. Which of the boys could you relate more to--Johnny or Juan? Explain your answer.

10. What is it "that must be encouraged and nurtured?"

11. Briefly explain in your own words the "two basic things one can do" to develop a grateful spirit.

    a.

    b.

12. What must happen to a woman "if she is going to be cleansed on the inside?"

13. Define love, "in simplest terms."

14. Having read the rest of the chapter, write down some ideas you might have about how you can get involved in helping others.

What the Scriptures Say

1. Read the following verses and write down what it is that God gives the believer.

Romans 6:23

II Peter 1:3

Matthew 16:19

Luke 10:19

2. Read Luke 11:37-44 and answer the following questions.

   According to verse 39 and what you know about the Pharisees, would you say that their outward lives were in order? Explain your answer.

   According to verse 40, would you say that Jesus thinks that what goes on inside a person is just as important as what they do outwardly? Explain your answer.

According to verse 43, what did the Pharisees love?

Can you see how the Pharisees had learned to do all of
the outward things to appear as though they were godly,
but in reality they had little love for God or others? What
does this story teach you about your own walk with God?

Personal Examination

1. What did you learn about overcoming lust from this chapter?

2. What did you learn about your own struggles from
this chapter?

Group Discussion Questions

1. What are some ways the spirit of this world can create an atmosphere conducive to sexual lust right in the home?
2. What can one do to maintain a spiritually clean environment at home?
3. As a group, come up with a list of thirty things you appreciate about your pastor (even if different churches are represented).
4. Can you see how selfishness can keep a person locked in sin?
5. As a group, make up a list of things that the women of the congregation could do around the church to be a blessing to the pastor and to others.

Study Questions

1. Take a few moments to read and consider the opening section of this chapter. Explain in your own words what your initial feelings are about God's judicial system.

2. Write out the definition of patience given by the *Theological Dictionary of the N.T.*

3. Complete the sentence which begins, "It is extremely dangerous…"

4. What is it "easy to get carried away with?"

5. What is "the dangerous thing about savoring God's love while in a state of unrepentant sin?"

6. Did Jesus' love for "the rich young ruler" determine his eternal destiny, or was it determined by "his response to that ardent love?" Explain your answer.

7. What is it that the authors are "convinced" of concerning grace?

8. According to John MacArthur, what "is not a genuine salvation?"

9. Write out the quote from the "old-time Baptist preacher."

10. What are "those who imagine that they can remain in unrepentant sin" really saying?

11. What is "very important for the woman whose life is characterized by lustful acts to know?"

What the Scriptures Say

1. Read the following verses and tell what you learn about sin.

    Matthew 5:28-29

    Galatians 5:19-21

I Corinthians 6:9-10

Hebrews 10:26-31

II Peter 2:20-21

I John 3:7-9

Read Luke 15:1-32 and answer the following questions.

What did the shepherd say in verse 6?

Write out what Jesus says about this in verse 7.

When the younger son finally came to an end of himself (in verse 19), how did the father respond in verse 20?

Personal Examination

1. What did you learn about God's grace from this chapter?

2. What did you learn about the way you have responded
   to that grace in the past from this chapter? What is your
   response now?

Group Discussion Questions

1. Read and discuss the fear of the Lord in the following verses:

    Proverbs 1:7

    Proverbs 3:7

    Proverbs 10:27

    Proverbs 14:26-27

    Proverbs 16:6

    Proverbs 19:23

    Proverbs 23:17

    Luke 12:5

ANSWERS

CHAPTER ONE

1. a. They were all professing Christians, and b. they all used sexual sin to gratify themselves. 2. While there are those women who are simply addicted to some type of sexual activity, most women involved in illicit sex use it as a means to attain some deeper form of satisfaction, such as the desire to feel love, be noticed, or even be desired sexually. 3. Your own answer. 4. Your own answer. 5. Jill deceived herself into believing that she was okay with the Lord. 6. a. 1992: 4%; b. 2005:11%.

CHAPTER TWO

1. Prince Charming rides into her life, rescues her from the villain (because, after all, her hero can't be a wimp!) and through it all, showers her with love and affection. It all began with watching animated movies. 2. This imaginary fairytale started her down the wrong road in her mind. Those kinds of scenarios [from animated movies] were permanently etched into her mind. 3. Certainly it is common and natural for the flesh, but this does not make it right, nor does it prove that purity of the mind is unattainable. 4. She became an aldulteress. 5. She was so needy for male affection that she felt lonely and unfulfilled if she wasn't receiving it. 6. Instead of entering marriage with a down-to-earth perspective about the normal struggles two young people will inevitably face, many new brides have lived in a fairytale fantasy for so long that the problems they should have been expecting, instead, seem insurmountable. 7. She assumed the honeymoon would last the rest of their lives. Even after Carl finally repented, Vicky was deeply resentful toward him and felt that he had destroyed what she had expected to be a perfect marriage. 8. Lie #32: "If I feel something, it must be true." Lie #33: "I can't control my emotions."

CHAPTER THREE

1.The truth is that prosperity and technological advances have simply made possible what women have always desired: the ability to make themselves look more beautiful. 2. Trendy shows such as *Friends, The OC, One Tree Hill*, and many others, are teaching girls to associate free, unrestrained sexual expression with success, happiness, power and "love." 3. There are 4 million cases of sexually transmitted diseases among teens annually. 4. Defense mechanisms are methods to cope with being hurt in life. Unfortunately, these defense mechanisms are the embryos of pride that begin in childhood, are developed in the teen years, and are perfected in adulthood. 5. She loved the feeling of power she had over a man when she teased him. 6. She was oblivious to the fact that she was causing guys at church to stumble into sin. 7. Lisa wanted a man who would worship her body. 8. They soon fall prey to the corruption of the atmosphere--hustling customers for drinks, prostitution, drug addiction, lesbianism, posing for pornographic photographs and performing unspeakable acts of perversion in stag movies.

CHAPTER FOUR

1. Each of these women had sexually unfulfilling marriages, and so they faced a very real challenge to maintain a pure heart and life. 2. The truth is that a woman will never have a pure heart as long as she vacillates about whether or not lust and masturbation are sinful. 3. The one who is

looking for the path of least resistance in life will also lack the determination to fight for a pure life. 4. Just as the physical heart pumps life-giving blood throughout the entire physiological being, so too the inner heart of man functions as the nucleus of all that goes on in a person's life. 5. a. "to set the heart upon, that is, long for" b. "sinful longing; the inward sin which leads to the falling away from God." c. "a longing for the unlawful, hence, concupiscence, desire, lust…the sensual desire connected with adultery, fornication." 6. a. First, there is *reactive* lust. This occurs when a good looking guy--or girl--comes into view. The woman's response may range from a quick glance to a longing, sinful gaze. b. What tends to be a greater issue with women is *proactive* lust. This occurs when the woman purposely uses the faculties of her mind for immoral purposes--with or without outside influence. 7. He faced a wall of unbelief that had formed from years of cold formalism. 8. He said exactly what He meant to say and it is very dangerous to put oneself in the position of explaining away His words. 9. For instance, if we are talking about a godly woman who "walks with the Lord," but then--in a moment of uncharacteristic weakness--succumbs to temptation and lusts or masturbates, but repents and gets back on track, that would rightly be termed *stumbling*. 10. The word stumble would not be the appropriate term to use for the woman who regularly indulges in lust or masturbation. 11. While occasions do exist wherein believers remain needlessly old-fashioned regarding particular issues, for the most part it seems that Christendom has become enormously contaminated by the sexualized culture in which we live, following one step behind an increasing wave of decadence. 12. Those who purpose to fill their lives with the temporal gratifications of this world view sex as simply one room in the vast pleasure palace of life.

CHAPTER FIVE

1. It all begins with temptation, moves into the person's particular routine, peaks in the actual act itself and ends with the lingering, inevitable consequences. 2. Promised fulfillment. 3. The craftiness of the enemy. 4. "A trigger is any event or emotion which evokes an inevitable response." 5. a. The actual temptation, b. the physical build-up, and c. opportunity. 6. Your own answer. 7. Because the woman sees only the instant gratification. 8. Forgetfulness of God. 9. Your own answer. 10. Rationalization. 11. Your own answer. 12. Your own answer. 13. Your own answer.

CHAPTER SIX

1. Your own answer. 2. The Bible clearly teaches the struggling woman to deal with her sinful nature. 3. The truth is, before a woman can ever hope to overcome habitual sin, she must first be willing to take responsibility for her *own* actions. 4. The first step toward victory over life-dominating habits is understanding that you are in your present circumstances because of the choices *you* have made for yourself. 5. One of the justifications we have heard over the years goes something like this: "My husband has just not been there for me and when a man at work started paying attention to me, I went to bed with him." 6. Since the roots of the person's problems lie in the realm of emotions, the counselor must help the counselee understand and deal with those issues before she will find freedom from her addiction. 7. In their minds, behind every human dilemma lies a complex combination of contributing factors that must be analyzed. 8. Habitual sexual sin is a by-product of a self-centered lifestyle. 9. God's purpose for His children is that they "become conformed to the image of His Son." 10. The woman walking in victory is one who has learned to "deny self." This must become a way of life. 11. Pride is simply being filled with self and a sense of one's own importance. 12. a. haughty spirit b. self-protective pride c. unapproachable pride d. vanity e. know-it-all pride f. self-exalting pride g. unsubmissive pride h. spiritual pride.

CHAPTER SEVEN

1. a. First, sexual sin is shameful to admit. b. Secondly, even though our society does not consider fornication or even adultery to be shameful, these sins are considered big "no-no's" in the evangelical movement. c. Another factor that contributes to a woman keeping her sin covered is that it is fairly easy to live a double life of outward religion and secret sexual sin. 2. Your own answer. 3. This is an extremely private place, an inner sanctum--a holy of holies, so to speak. 4. Your own answer. 5. a. Presumably it begins on the playground where kids can be so cruel to one another. b. The fear is deepened during the awkward teenage years, c. and becomes embedded during adulthood. 6. In essence, they ignore the importance of the inward life and choose to concentrate on presenting the most favorable outward appearance. 7. That she has no sin. 8. God loves her too much to allow her to maintain her secret sin. 9. Your own answer. 10. Keeping herself hyped up in a false sense of security will only keep her buried under the burden of unconfessed sin, which in turn will further the delusion about her spirituality. 11. Your own answer. 12. Your own answer.

CHAPTER EIGHT

1. a. Through a miracle, which occurs instantaneously, or b. through a process of change over an extended period of time. 2. Through a gradual, well-organized process of transforming the woman into a new creation. 3. One of the things we must realize is that if God were to instantly set us free, it would then be much easier for us to return to old habits. 4. Your own answer. 5. God is often more concerned about exposing and expelling the underlying issues of the heart than He is about the outward sin with which she struggles. 6. a. Will my selfishness simply be transferred to spending money? b. Will I live out the rest of my life with no concern for the lost who are going to hell around me? c. Will I continue to be self-centered with my family? 7. A life transformed from one of corruption and utter uselessness to one of fruitfulness and purpose. 8. a. surmount, b. prevail against, c. subjugate, d. master, and e. overpower. 9. Your own answer. 10. a. Has she been doing it for years? b. Has she been in denial over her problem? c. Has she been refusing to face responsibility for her actions? d. How deep has she gone into depravity? The answers to these questions are your own. 11. Your own answer.

CHAPTER NINE

1. Your own answer. 2. You may have blamed others for your problems for years, but now it is time to get tough and be determined to beat this thing with the strength and power of God! 3. Your own answer. 4. Your own answer. 5. Persistence in prayer. 6. Your own answer. 7. Christ. 8. Who He is. 9. The unbelief that it fosters. 10. Your own answer.

CHAPTER TEN

1. a. The flesh, b. the world, and c. the enemy. 2. God wants married couples, whom He has enjoined, to enjoy each other--thus, He made sex a pleasurable experience. 3. An alcoholic could go through her entire life without ever handling another drink, but a sex addict must learn to control her appetites. 4. a. Comfort, b. pleasure, and c. the preservation of self. 5. A corrupted nature bent toward sin. 6. Heart, soul, mind, spirit, inward parts. 7. Through the five senses (touch, taste, see, hear, and smell). 8. Just as the flesh grows stronger when we feed it with sensuous living, our spirit grows stronger when it is nourished with the things of God. 9. a. If we practice (or sow) ungodliness then we will desire (or reap) more ungodliness. b. By the same token, if we practice godliness then we will desire a greater godliness, and c. Feelings always follow behavior. 10. Our own fallen nature.

CHAPTER ELEVEN

1. With such overwhelming exposure as this, why should anyone be surprised that a young teenager indulges in sex? 2. "The carnal world would have us believe that pleasure is the only purpose of sex. Some prudish Christians think that pleasure has nothing to do with sex. Both are wrong." 3. To *separate* ourselves from the world. 4. That is just not true. Satan is subtle—he develops attitudes slowly. 5. Your own answers. 6. Network television. 7. These words create an image of a soldier standing on guard duty, expecting to be attacked by enemy forces at any moment -- completely alert. 8. Rather than aggressively tearing down the strongholds of the enemy and waging war for the souls of our loved ones, we have allowed the enemy to ravage, plunder and exploit us. Instead of affecting the world around us for the cause of Christ, we have allowed this world's system to dictate our lives.

CHAPTER TWELVE

1. Your own answer. 2. To the one who struggles with depression, a devil of dark gloom would be appointed. For those who battle a hot temper, a spirit of rage or murder would be given the task; and for an exaggerated sex drive, an unclean spirit would be commissioned. 3. Your own answer. 4. Your own answer. 5. That the person who *habitually* transgresses God's laws is in league with Satan -- the great rebel himself. 6. The result is always an increased degree of demon influence. 7. Your own answer. 8. Your own answer. 9. Those who have become accustomed to losing spiritual battles. 10. Your own answer.

CHAPTER THIRTEEN

1. God changes people from the inside out. 2. This change occurs as the woman sees her need for change, comes to grip with her sinful behavior, and experiences a genuine turning away from that lifestyle. 3. A tremendous upheaval of her entire inner life is necessary. 4. For a woman to believe that she can repent of some particular sin without changing her way of thinking. 5. *Spiritual repentance is an experience whereby a person's will is altered for the express purpose of bringing it into line with God's will.* 6. Your own answer. 7. The transforming of a woman from being one who does her own (carnal) will, to one who does the will of her Father. 8. Your own answer. 9. Your own answer. 10. Your own answer.

CHAPTER FOURTEEN

1. A person who does not heed instruction nor receive "the life-giving reproof." 2. Your own answer. 3. Your own answer. 4. Between the wise and the foolish. 5. That Peter would learn to discern the difference between the voice of the Holy Spirit and the voice of the enemy. 6. Sometimes a sharp rebuke is the very thing we need to get us back on track -- to bring us down off our "high horse," so to speak. 7. The words of a man who had been through the process of God's correction for over thirty years. 8. The woman who will be loosed from sin must exhibit the character of someone who has indeed been set free. 9. Some women in sexual sin see their sin as a minor quirk in an otherwise impeccable character. 10. Holiness comes by the Lord's purging out of us our love for sin and for self.

CHAPTER FIFTEEN

1. She must learn to walk in the Spirit. 2. "IF... ye walk in the Spirit, THEN... ye shall not fulfill the lust of the flesh" 3. Lifestyle. 4. An ongoing condition of a person's life. 5. Your own answers. 6. One problem people in sexual sin face is that their thinking has been warped by the enemy. 7. Getting God's Word on the inside to saturate our lives, thoughts, attitudes, emotions, and actions, so that we are conformed from the inside out into the

likeness of Jesus Christ. 8. The importance of soaking up God's Word.

CHAPTER SIXTEEN

1. Take some drastic measures. 2. Spiritual atmospheres conducive to lust. 3. In practical terms, the spirit of this world capitalizes upon the fact that humans have carnal desires which are innate within them: the lust for pleasure, the lust for gain, and the lust for position. 4. a. "…the mall…provokes people to want more and mor and more." b. "Beauty salons are notorious for their carnal atmospheres." and c. "…a bar, the ambience puts her in a partying mood." 5. She must do everything within her power to minimize the enemy's ability to affect her spiritually. 6. Lustful living is hellish living. 7. Learning to be thankful. 8. "Look at all I have! Thank You Lord, for all that You have done for me and given me. I don't need anything else." 9. Your own answer. 10. Gratitude is a disposition of the heart. 11. Your own answer. 12. A transformation will have to take place within. 13. To give of oneself. 14. Your own answer.

CHAPTER SEVENTEEN

1. Your own answer. 2. "The majestic God graciously restrains his righteous wrath, as in his saving work for Israel…He does so in covenant faithfulness but also out of regard for human frailty…Forbearance, of course, is not renunciation but postponement with a view to repentance." 3. It is extremely dangerous for a woman involved in habitual sin to assume that because she has not yet had her "day of reckoning" for her misconduct that there will be no forthcoming judgment to face. 4. The feelings produced by God's love and to corrupt it into something it is not meant to be. 5. A woman can actually be deceived, thinking she is in true fellowship with the Lord. 6. Your own answer. 7. What many people today are accepting as grace is really nothing more than *the presumptuous license to sin.* 8. "Any 'salvation' that does not alter a lifestyle of sin and transform the heart of the sinner." 9. "That's like the unrepentant thief who went before the judge pleading not to be sent to prison. He had no intention of quitting the behavior that got him into his predicament. He only wanted to be spared a prison sentence." 10. *"I don't want to be cleansed; I just want to be forgiven."* 11. As much as she has indulged in sin, God has an even greater measure of grace to overcome that sin.

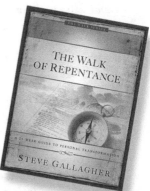
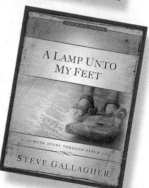

PURE LIFE MINISTRIES

BIBLICAL TEACHING MATERIALS
Pure Life offers a full line of books, DVDs and CDs specifically designed to supply Christians with the tools they need to live in sexual purity.

INNOVATIVE WEB SITE
Our web site features a searchable archive of inspirational articles, a weekly podcast, compelling audio messages, blogs, testimonies and more.

SPEAKING MINISTRY
The members of the PLM Speaking Team are equipped to address a number of issues in various settings: men's conferences on purity, teaching seminars for pastors and counselors, single adult and youth events, and ministry to women, wives or couples.

PRISON MINISTRY
PLM empowers prison chaplains by sending several thousand complimentary books into prisons every year. We also teach weekly classes through *At the Altar of Sexual Idolatry* in several sex offender facilities.

COUNSELING MINISTRY
• *Residential Care* - The most intense and involved counseling the staff offers comes through the Live-in Program (55 beds, 6-12 months), conducted on the 45-acre PLM campus in Kentucky. The godly and sober atmosphere at Pure Life Ministries provokes the hunger for God and deep repentance that destroys the hold of sin in men's lives.

• *Help At Home* - The Overcomers At-Home Program is a twelve-week counseling program which features weekly counseling sessions and many of the same teachings offered in the Live-in Program. This program is available for women who struggle with sexual sin, as well as struggling men and their wives.

• *Counseling Help Line* - Our Counseling Help Line is available to people facing critical life decisions. This service is intended to assist them in choosing the right course of action.

• *Counseling Staff* - All of our male and female counselors hold degrees and are trained in biblical counseling and certified by the International Association of Biblical Counselors.

For more information about Pure Life Ministries, visit our web site at www.purelifeministries.org or call 888.PURELIFE.